SEARCH
TOGEThⅭⴽ

MW00422852

Originally founded in 1972 as the *Baptist Reformation Review*, *Searching Together* is a journal published quarterly by Quoir. Thanks primarily to the work of Jon and Dotty Zens—and the support of various volunteers and groups over the years—this publication has sought to stir up the body of Christ, challenge thought, create dialogue, encourage, and build up the followers of Christ far and wide.

Since 1982, *Searching Together* has carried on with the founding thought of the first editor, Norbert Ward: "[We] make no claim to be the voice of a movement or an organized denomination. We do not, on the other hand, claim to be a lone voice. We believe that we are expressing the hope and earnest prayer of concerned believers."

Over the years, *Searching Together* has focused on the themes of the life of Christ in His body, getting along with one another, and the implications of being the Bride of Christ in a fallen culture. We long to be saturated with the cry of Paul's heart—"the love of Christ compels me..." Herman Ridderbos emphasized that the Gospel finds its most central and fundamental expression in love. "In the first place, this love derives its central significance from the fact that it is the reflection of the love of God in Jesus Christ. The love of God revealed in Christ's self-surrender and working itself out by the Holy Spirit in the love of the church is the real secret and clearest expression of its holiness."

We trust that this issue of *Searching Together* will encourage you in the love of Christ.

EDITOR
Jon Zens

ST TEAM
Greta Bemisderfer
James Berling
Timothy Bolton
Bobbye Bower
Kat Huff
Bonnie & Gary Jaeckle
Shamra & Dale Martin
Rafael Polendo
Teighlor Polendo
Arlan Purdy
Jodi & Marv Root
Heather Toftness
Charlene Wilder

PUBLISHER
Quoir
Orange, CA
quoir.com

**COVER DESIGN &
INTERIOR LAYOUT**
Rafael Polendo
polendo.net

ISBN
978-0-9913345-4-4

**VOLUME 41:03-04
FALL/WINTER 2015**

SUBSCRIPTION INFO

SUBSCRIPTIONS

A subscription to *Searching Together* is available for $10 per year (United Kingdom £2 per issue). Discounts and free subscriptions are available to those who cannot afford the full subscription price. A discount of $7 per year is available for subscriptions involving five or more copies to the same address. A set of back issues from 1978 to present can be ordered from *Searching Together* for $70 postpaid. We will send a gift subscription to anyone from you for $5 per year.

INQUIRIES AND CORRESPONDENCE

If you want to reprint an article, please write to *Searching Together* for permission and include *Searching Together's* address in the credits. Articles may be reproduced for small-scale distribution without permission. Correspondence to authors should be sent to *Searching Together*.

CONTACT INFORMATION

United States
Searching Together/Jon Zens
P.O. Box 548, St. Croix Falls,
WI 54024
jzens@searchingtogether.org
(715) 338-2796
www.searchingtogether.org

Australia
Ray Levick
Unit 25, 61-67 Moverly Rd.
Maroubra 3035 Australia
rlevick@netspace.net.au

Canada
Larry Hartley
2391 Route 114
Weldon, N.B.
Canada E4H 4R2
chegutu@nbnet.nb.ca

United Kingdom
Siobhan & Mike O'Leary
Beulah Print & Design
19 Fair Street
Drogheda Co, Louth, Ireland

CONTENTS

MORE FROM JON ZENS

- Dispensationalism: An Inquiry Into Its Leading Figures & Features, 1978

- Desiring Unity...Finding Division: Lessons from the 19th Century Restoration Movement, 1986

- Moses In the Millennium: An Analysis of Christian Reconstructionism, 1988

- This Is My Beloved Son, Hear Him: The Foundation of New Covenant Ethics & Ecclesiology, 1997

- A Church Building Every 1/2 Mile: What Makes American Christianity Tick? 2008

- What's With Paul & Women? Unlocking the Cultural Background to 1 Timothy 2, 2011

- No Will of My Own: How Patriarchy Smothers Female Dignity & Personhood, 2011

- Christ Minimized? A Response to Rob Bell's Love Wins, 2012

- The Pastor Has No Clothes: Moving from Clergy-Centered Church to Christ-Centered Ekklesia, 2012

- To Preach or Not to Preach? The Church's Urgent Question (David C. Norrington with Replies to the Critics & an Introduction by Jon Zens), 2013

- 58 to 0: How Christ Leads Through the One Anothers, 2013

WWW.JONZENS.COM

CHRIST ALONE: FIVE CHALLENGES EVERY GROUP WILL FACE

JON ZENS

Because of their spiritual DNA in Christ, believers instinctively want to be with one another. As a result of this reality, there are groups of Christ-followers all over the earth. Brothers and sisters love being together!

As we all know, groups of Jesus' family are not utopias. Just like in physical families, spiritual families face challenges.

I would like to look at five *foundational* challenges that every group needs to address. If those in the group are not on the same page concerning these perspectives when a group is birthed, it is likely that their life together will not last long, or they may continue together and later fall back into institutional patterns.

1. THE CHALLENGE FOR CHRIST TO BE EVERYTHING

The tricky issue is that every believing group states that they wish for Christ to be at the center. However, there is evidence to suggest that Jesus is not the heart-throb of many non-institutional gatherings. Why? Because there must be a revelation from Father in order for an individual and a community to embrace His eternal purpose to glorify the Son in all things.

Frank Viola has beautifully captured the "one page" which everyone must be on in order for Christ to functionally be the End-all Be-all of an *Ekklesia*.

In so many modern churches, a set of doctrines, a certain theology, a charismatic personality, a set of special works or ministries, is the centrality rather than Christ. Mark it down: The centrality of anything other than Christ is a betrayal of the new species.

All of the churches and movements I was involved in had effectively preached to me an "it." Evangelism is an "it." The power of God is an "it." Eschatology is an "it." Christian theology is an "it." Christian doctrine is an "it." Faith is an "it." Apologetics is an "it." Healing and deliverance are "its."

I made the striking discovery that I don't need an "it." I have never needed an "it." And I will never need an "it." Christian "its," no matter how good or true, eventually wear out, run dry, and become tiresome.

I don't need an "it," I need a Him!

God's object, from first to last, is His Son. It is Christ—and Christ alone—that God the Father desires for His people. I had grossly confused spiritual growth with acquiring spiritual things. So I went about pursuing spiritual knowledge, spiritual virtues, spiritual graces, spiritual gifts, and spiritual power. I later discovered that spiritual growth is nothing more than having Christ formed within (Gal. 4:19).

As I survey the landscape of modern Christianity, it seems to me that spiritual things and objects have replaced the person of Christ. The doctrines, gifts, graces, virtues, and duties that we so earnestly seek have been substituted for Jesus Himself. We look to this gift and that gift, we study this truth and that truth, we seek to appropriate this virtue, we try to fulfill this duty, but all along we fail to find Him.

When the Father gives us something, it's always His Son. When the Son gives us something, it's always Himself.[1]

Brothers and sisters, what is being said here gets to the heart of Who we are about. If Christ is not the warp-and-woof of our being, we might as well fold up and return to the institutional system.

"Spiritual things and objects have replaced the person of Christ." This is the key to understanding why so many groups—both institutional and non-institutional—peter out, split, spin wheels, go off on tangents, look to 'leaders' to keep them going, and end up leaving people in confusion and a world of hurt. I've heard many say things like, "Oh, I was in a house church for a season, but it folded," and "I had a bad experience in a simple church."

Here is a concrete example that recently came to me from a friend who was in a home group that dissolved.

> I was in a very small group. This house gathering was a big disappointment in that they put out brochures/flyers in public places saying *anyone and everyone was welcome*. We had a man for a while who would only say "Yeshua," and did not have any regard for the teachings of Paul. But *they kept welcoming him back!* We got people who only could share their personal concerns. Their family issues became the priority, and they had an agenda to relocate that involved finding a *boat to live on out of the country*, using money from an inheritance. I think this group was far from Ekklesia, even though I stayed with it for some time.

This is the reason groups fail and disintegrate: *their being together is not about Christ, but things.* I fear that in too many cases Jesus is an *assumption* behind what a group does, but He is not functionally the Living Vine, the Loving Leader of it. I love the way one Ekklesia expressed their reason for being: "Learning together to live by the indwelling life of Christ."

It is critical that communities move forward and build on the foundation of Christ. It cannot be assumed that just because a group starts fresh that they function with Christ as the Cornerstone. That is why most groups would do well to consider having experienced outside help in their desire to grow as branches rooted in the Vine.

Paul came among people with a One-Person agenda. "I was not in your midst as one stringing great words together. Rather, I determined to know nothing among you except Jesus Christ, and Him as crucified."

Communities cannot begin by "knowing nothing" but Christ, and then move on to other things as time elapses. Life together is "knowing nothing" but Christ day in and day out.

2. THE CHALLENGE TO TRUST CHRIST AS LEADER

A brochure promoting a conference put on by the Willow Creek Church in Illinois announced, "Thousands of leaders across North America gather together to hear speakers from all over the world, participate in interactive dialogue, and have practical training— which focuses on helping the church raise up leaders, as well as helping leaders in churches develop their leadership gifts."

The truth is, since 250 AD the visible church has been all about leaders. If you read church histories, the great bulk of the content is about this leader and that leader. It cannot be denied that what church has been about is "leadership." The thousands of books about leadership and the many aspects of "pastoral leadership" testify loudly to the lop-sided emphasis on this subject that dominates the church landscape.

Jesus, however, did not share our inherited views about leadership. When talking about the religious leaders of His day, He noted that they liked to be greeted publicly as "Rabbi, Rabbi" (in our day it would be "Reverend, Reverend"). Christ told His audience, "don't be called 'Rabbi,' for I alone am your Teacher, and you are all brothers and sisters."

He went on to assert, "don't call anyone 'Father' on earth, for One is your Father in heaven. Neither be called 'leaders,' for One is your Leader, the Anointed One. The greatest among you will be the one who takes care of others."

Jesus told us rather clearly not to be called "leaders," yet the history of the church is mostly about people wanting positions with titles so that they can be set above others as "leaders." Even in groups meeting outside mainline churches, the emphasis often still falls on "leaders," and much energy is devoted to continually training more non-leaders to become "leaders."

How can we expect it to be clear that Jesus is our Leader when we spend so much time focusing on human leaders? Our Lord specifically said that calling humans "leaders" would detract and deflect from His singular Leadership. Typical concerns about "leaders" should never be an issue in organic groups. Function together for a period of time as a priesthood of all believers, and see what He reveals in your life together down the pike.

"How Does God Develop Leaders?"

The topic of "leadership" comes up all the time in groups on Facebook. In this instance I responded, and my thoughts speak to why worrying about leadership is vastly premature in believing groups.

[David Munley:] *In your view, how does God develop leaders?*

[Jon:] Given the flow of church history and the accretion of assumptions, this is a question with many layers of concerns that could be addressed.

But in a nutshell, I would say that Father is not focused on developing leaders. His purpose is to see Christ formed in His people. When believers function as simply brothers and sisters in a community for a length of time, the expression of Christ and specific aspects of giftedness blossom in His Bride.

It is my observation that this is the crucial dimension absent from the great majority of "church leaders." They have rarely lived out the life of Christ in the body for sustained periods of time as non-leaders. The NT speaks about "knowing" one another. This reality comes only through long-term relationships. A huge problem is that many leaders are not "known."

CHRIST ALONE | SEARCHING TOGETHER

You know a person when you've seen them function in all the vicissitudes of life as a brother or sister.

As I said in *58 to 0–How Christ Leads Through the One Anothers*: "In the NT, the organic way for everything to develop is through the functioning of all the living stones together. To focus on leaders without having first a functioning body is to put the proverbial cart before the horse–with far-reaching dire consequences. If a group is filled with Jesus and his guidance, 'leaders' will probably not be on their minds; if a group lacks the fullness of Jesus, they will probably become fixated on the need for 'leaders.'"

[Billie Ritter Ford:] *I think a leader is one who steps out ahead of the group and says 'let's try it this way.'*

[Jon:] That's true, but what many miss is that anyone in the body can say, "let's try this." Everyone participates in the Spirit's leadership. We are used to just looking at a few as "leaders." But the Lord brings leadership out of all the saints as time goes on—if the open opportunity and loving atmosphere are present. Spirit-leadership can be seen as shifting and floating among the whole priesthood.[2]

"Hear My Son"

Father removed Moses and Elijah from the scene, and when the three disciples looked up, they saw only Jesus, and the voice from the Shekinah glory proclaimed, "This is My beloved Son, hear Him." How could our One focus be any clearer?

The body of Christ must listen to the Lord. Each person in the body, and the body as a whole is able to hear the Son's voice. We want to hear from our Leader. In order for His leadership to prosper among us, we must stop looking to one or a few, and cease calling people "leaders."

"We Want a King"

Israel came to a point where they wanted a human king like the nations around them had. They were not satisfied with a King who ruled and provided without being seen. They desired a tangible, visible king to protect and to watch over them. This was a sinful request, but the Lord granted it to them.

I believe resident in almost all of us is that same desire for a fleshly king. We'd love to just have someone give us a grocery list of what to do, what not to do, what to believe, what to think—and pay them to spoon-feed us!

With every fiber of grace in our being we must resist the temptation to have a human king! Instead, we must all see ourselves as part of Christ's leadership in His body. He gives each part a manifestation of the Spirit for the common good.

Common Questions

"Can a community function without human leaders?"
Absolutely. Christ must be trusted as an all-sufficient Leader. Leadership takes place in every group. The vital issue is this: *is it by the Spirit through all the parts, or induced by the flesh in one or a few parts?* If there are "go-to" persons in a group who the others assume will get things started, maybe do some teaching, and generally keep the meeting going, then that group is already headed down the wrong path. If a community is driven by the ideas and preferences of one or a few, it is not going to be driven by Christ flowing through the whole body.

"Isn't leadership needed?"
Absolutely. The big problem is that Jesus' leadership gets lost in the shuffle. The leadership that is needed is *His*, but we are so used to defaulting to specific human leaders (whether they have titles or not) that Christ's oversight is marginalized. The ideal is for His guidance to be expressed through all the parts by the Spirit. Again, if a group is fixated on Christ, the issue of leadership will fade into the background.

"Doesn't someone have to be in charge?"
Absolutely. Someone already is in charge, and that someone is Jesus Christ. Are we totally satisfied to rest in His Leadership, or will we cave into the fleshly desire to have human kings? Obviously, churches have had leaders "in charge" for hundreds of years, and their track record is deplorable. There simply is no evidence to suggest that assemblies thrive in Christ when the clergy are in charge.

"Without a pastor's presence and vision, won't there be chaos?"
Heavy centralization of power in "the pastor" has been going on for centuries and church folk know well that chaos has not been averted. Chaos occurs many times daily in American churches. "Knowing nothing" but Jesus Christ is the only way to avoid chaos in a community. Pursuing the 58 "one anothers" in our shared life in Christ together will go a long way toward helping us experience deep love, not chaos.

"Didn't Paul talk about elders and deacons?"
Yes. But compared to the early church our conceptions and practice of these terms is totally disconnected. Back then, giftedness developed in a relational family setting over a long period of time. The saints were "known" by each other. Now, we have turned things into offices and positions, the family dimension has been lost for the most part, and often people are placed into leadership without being "known." Tradition has separated "the pastor" from other elders, and this has created a whole set of further difficulties and problems.

The following response to my blog post, "The One-Person System Strikes Again," pretty much summarizes our current state of affairs regarding Christ as our Leader:

Jon, you said, "There is already Someone to lead congregations, and His name is Jesus Christ." Sadly, when I was part of an attempt to re-think the way we were doing church, I was told, "Anything with more than one head is a monster." I tried to point out that we already had one head—Jesus—and so in fact it was we, ourselves, who were creating a monster. Guess who was "encouraged" out of the church....

Trusting Jesus to lead His flock is tough, no doubt. It is risky, and it is vulnerable. Most of us are so used to a church bulletin telling us what is next. In contrast, laying down all our agendas and expectations, and committing everything to Him as the Great Shepherd is the way to open up His life flowing freely through the saints. "'Tis so sweet to trust in Jesus." Do we really believe that?

"It ain't faith until you're out of answers

It ain't faith until you've got no plan

It ain't faith until you're standing in the middle

Of what you will never understand."[3]

3. THE CHALLENGE TO DEEPEN RELATIONSHIPS

The 58 "one anothers" in the New Testament—such as love one another, encourage one another, be long-suffering with one another—imply ongoing relationships. The New Testament envisions believers to be in fellowship with others in their locale.

Excitement rises in many hearts as they look forward to open, participatory gatherings where Christ expresses Himself through many. As wonderful as such meetings can be, they are in fact only part of the picture. In light of "encouraging one another daily," it is important that brothers and sisters deepen relationships, as much as they are able to, every day of the week.

Getting to know one another better is vital. It can happen in scads of ways—over coffee, over meals, watching a movie, going to a sports event, having a picnic together, praying together, reading together, etc., etc. The possibilities are endless.

The pursuit of relationships in the body must be intentional, yet natural and organic. It must not be forced, manufactured or induced by guilt. In light of the importance of our shared life in Christ together, it would seem wise for a group to come together periodically to discuss how things are going along these lines.

We all know there are serious obstacles to our pursuit of deepening relationships.

- There are *geographical* challenges

- There are *personal* challenges

- There are *family* challenges

- There are *work* challenges

- There are a host of *cultural* challenges

The list could go on. However, in spite of all the obstacles, if the brothers and sisters are serious about going deeper in the Lord with one another, you would be amazed at what creative ways He can reveal for the body to enhance their mutual fellowship. This can happen if they come together, honestly put their cards on the table, and ask Jesus for help. "In Christ" relationships simply do not deepen without Spirit-led intentionality.

To assume that all will be well by coming together once a week is a disaster lurking in the bushes. Some groups may have geographical challenges that allow them to only come together once a week. If that is the case, then it might be possible to turn it into an all day affair in which relationships could be cultivated through a variety of activities.

When the bumpy times come, shallow, superficial relationships will not cut it. The better people come to know and understand each other, the better they can handle the difficult seasons that any family will face in their life together. Larry Crabb pinpoints how crucial ongoing body-life is:

Change takes place when truth is presented in relationship. Perhaps a relationship of deep regard and empathetic concern is the context for change, creating an atmosphere in which the truth of God can be heard non-defensively and thus penetrate more deeply . . . . To be a healthy church, truth must be presented in the context of encouraging relationships.[4]

Encouraging relationships do not occur automatically. To highlight this truth, I think of a story Bruce Olson told in his book, *Bruchko*. The people in the Motilone tribe in Columbia moved from place to place together in the jungle, they hunted together, they slept in the same quarters together, and they ate together. Yet they had no *loving relationships* with each other. They were cold to one another. They went through their tasks together stoically as duties to perform in order to survive. This illustrates that people can even be in each other's faces 24/7 and still have no vital connection as human beings. It was not until Christ blossomed in this tribe that loving relationships began to be cultivated.

Every group has its nuances and unique circumstances. I would encourage believing communities to bring the 58 "one anothers" before the Lord and ask Him how Jesus' ways can further prosper among the saints as the Spirit leads.

"A Community of . . . ."

As a general encouragement to pursue, value and nurture relationships, I'd like to set before you an edited version of a body-statement issued in 1979 by Salem Community Church in Massachusetts.

"We are a community of *forgiveness*. We will fail each other many times, but we wish to forgive and love one another in spite of our failings.

We are a community of *acceptance*. Our love for one another cannot be based on performance, but on an unconditional acceptance of each other in Christ.

We are a community of *availability*. All that we have we want to use to serve others and meet their needs.

We are a community of *prayer*. We will pray for each other before Father with regularity.

We are a community of *openness*. We have agreed to be more open persons, disclosing our feelings, struggles, joys and hurts to one another. We need each other, we need mutual trust, and we need honesty in our dealings with each other.

We are a community of *sensitivity*. We desire to be sensitive to one another, to seek and know and understand each other to the best of our ability.

We are a community of *service*. We reject a prideful, self-centered view of life, and seek to become people who find joy in service.

We are a community of *accountability*. We want to intertwine our lives with one another. We know that what any member does affects the others deeply, so we seek to discuss major decisions corporately, rather than in isolation from our brothers and sisters."

4. THE CHALLENGE TO BE DEFINED BY CHRIST, NOT ADAM

Many have been convinced of things they are not,
and this prevents them from being convinced of what they truly are.
(Terrance Williams, Facebook, July, 2015)

Believers can be viewed from many angles in the New Testament, but certainly the pivotal one is that they are "in Christ," and as such are fully adopted by Father and free from condemnation. Our starting point must be that our standing and righteousness are in Christ alone. As the old hymn put it, "Nothing in our hands we bring, simply to Your cross we cling."

There are many -isms, teachings and voices that undermine Christ as sufficient in redemption. We must resist these, as Paul did, and take our stand on the free grace of the Lord Jesus Christ. We must see ourselves as the Lord does—a New Creation, a New Humanity, a spotless Bride, and as those who died with Christ on the cross, were buried with Him, and raised from death to sit with Christ in heavenly places. Frank Viola's words give us cause to exult in Jesus alone:

> Paul's life was spent trying to extinguish the specific falsehoods that eroded the notion that God's demeanor toward us is grace-full. His letters throb with countless "blame-extinguishing" declarations. These explosive statements are designed to inoculate the church from any accusation that can be laid at her feet. "There is no condemnation to those in Christ Jesus."
>
> God accepts only one person, His beloved Son. And we are in Him, which means He accepts us on exactly the same basis as He accepts Christ. Therefore, we need not struggle to earn God's favor. We only need to come to Christ and rest in Him.
>
> God's object from first to last is His Son. It is Christ—and Christ alone—that God the Father desires for His people.
>
> When the Father gives us something, it's always His Son. When the Son gives us something, it's always Himself.
>
> *The early Christians saw themselves as truly being "in Christ."* They were pulled loose from a "works" mentality, liberated from a guilt complex, and set free from a sense of religious duty.
>
> This was reflected in their conversation. If you open up the New Testament letters, you will find that Paul always addressed the churches he planted (despite what they were going through) with the arresting phrase "holy ones." He saw them as holy "in Christ."
>
> A sister in one of the churches I worked with stood up in a meeting and gave a testimony. She said, "I have been raised a

Christian since I was a child. I've been meeting with you all for about a year now. I was listening to the Christian radio, as I sometimes do, and a song came on. The singer was singing about how unworthy she was and how she needed to try harder to please God. She sang that her righteousness was as filthy rags, and she needed to improve her spiritual walk.

I paused and suddenly realized that I couldn't relate to that song anymore. I couldn't relate to it because I've been given new eyes to see myself in Christ. For many years I struggled with a sense of unworthiness, guilt, and condemnation. But that's all gone now. I don't have it anymore, and I feel so free in the Lord's love!"

When she shared this testimony, the room erupted and others began to testify along the same lines. It was an awesome experience. I believe this sister had touched the early Christian mind. She was laying hold of the same spiritual reality that the early Christians laid hold of.

Who we are in Christ is beautifully explored and unfolded in Milt Rodriguez's *The Butterfly in You: Discovering Your True Identity in Christ*. It is a read that might possibly shake your world and could bring you to see the glories of Christ in you.

I would like to point out two connected lines of thought that muddy the waters and keep the believer locked in the old Adam, instead of flowing in the liberty of our Lord, the Last Adam.

"The good that I would do, I don't do"

These words from Romans 7 are usually misquoted and misused, bringing untold confusion to believers. Let's think about some highlights in Paul's line of thought here.

His audience is specified—"I speak to those who know the law." He's speaking here to Jews familiar with the law, not Gentiles. The setting Paul has in mind is also specific—"when we [Jews] were in the flesh . . . ." From the get-go it is clear that he has a pre-Christ perspective in mind.

Yet, ignoring the people and the context Paul had in mind, many teachers assume that Romans 7 is about "the normal" believing life. Thus, when they come to these words—"what I want to do, I don't do; what I hate, that I do; I am fleshy, sold under sin"—they assume that we have here the inevitable battle of the believer, rather than of a Jew struggling under the Law.

This view has a number of problems. Here are a few. First, the "good" spoken of here in chapter 7 refers to the Law, not Gospel good works flowing out of the believer from Christ. Second, "fleshy, sold under sin" cannot be a definition of a saint because these verses are sandwiched between the strongest statements by Paul in chapters 6 and 8 that sin cannot lord it over (have dominion over) him/her, and that there is no condemnation to those in Christ. The person in chapter 7 is a slave to sin; the person in chapter 8 is not a debtor to live after the flesh.

For the most part, in Roman Catholicism and Protestantism Romans 7 has been the center point of the believer's life. This being the case, you can see why church people have found their identity more with Adam than Christ. For example, "what I want to do, I don't do" was the mantra of the Puritan view of sanctification in the 17th and 18th centuries. Thus, this view was embedded in British Christianity and then imported into New England by the Puritans.

You can see why the evangelicalism/fundamentalism that emerged in America since the 19th century has leaned toward defining believers more by their connection to Adam than to the Last Adam.

Sin Management

The Puritan view that sin still clings to any good actions by believers is debilitating. Still holding up the Law as the standard is retrogressive and forgets that "law is the strength of sin."

Because of various factors in the development of American Christianity, the focus of the preaching and teaching in the 19th and 20th centuries came to fall on what was considered right and wrong behavior, with "the good I would do, I do not; but the evil I would not do, I do" being an oft-used proof-text.

Paul Lehmann said in his *Ethics in a Christian Context* (1963), the focus of the Gospel is "not morality, but maturity," growing up into Christ. In the American scene there was too much eating from the tree of good and evil, which unfortunately led to feasting on Christ as the Tree of Life being lost in the cracks.

It would appear that a great deal of church teaching fosters compulsive concern for morality, but there is little attention directed to Jesus' key image that we must bear fruit by resting in Him, and that we can do nothing without Him bringing it forth from us. A former Filipino pastor, Bong Manayon, told of a time he got a phone call at 2am from a young man he knew who was in a disco club needing help. Bong went in and rescued him out of bad situation. Then he realized that the people he churched with would likely condemn him for going into a club, and be would more focused on that than the needs of the young man.

The believer's life is in Christ. Christ came to begin a New Creation, not to patch up an old creation. We must resist the human traditions that focus on Adam and sin. Our life, our being, is Christ. Period.

5. THE CHALLENGE TO LET THE LOVE OF CHRIST REIGN

Years ago Vernon Grounds wrote a great article, "The Fellowship of Porcupines." In it, he noted that we are all capable of poking each other! This being true, Paul directed believers to "forgive one another as God in Christ forgave you."

When you boil it down, we can all be tough nuts to crack. We are like a bunch of crooked, gnarly sticks put in a bundle, and what holds us together is the scarlet cord of Christ's love. Our heart's desire should be to see the love of Christ flowing freely through us, His body. But the sad reality is that at the drop of a hat we can violate the bonds of love.

Paul was not shocked that believers had problems with each other, but he was grieved when they did not follow the direction of Jesus' love to repair the issues. Paul summarized our walk with Jesus with these simple, but profound words, *"live a life of love."* Here, I would like to talk about what is on my heart concerning the outworking of God's love in His body.

Humility and Brokenness

First of all, I think we would all agree that many problems surface because the saints lack humility. This word literally means "low to the ground," not in the sense of being a groveling worm, but in the sense of not exalting oneself. "In order to listen to others we need to be humble, small in our own estimation. Finding the solution to a math problem is possible without humility, but finding God's will is impossible without this virtue" (Thomas Dubay). A humble person is wide open to the Lord, listens to others, defers to others, is detached from their agendas, and intentionally seeks to put others ahead of themselves.

A room full of humble people is a powerful environment. Pride, however, will ruin the whole clump of dough.

Healing

Life is hard. Many have wounds, hurts and scars—some very deep—from their journey. As they come into the body of Christ, they should find a setting of love, acceptance and care where a process of healing can begin.

> "Every healthy group is therapeutic . . . . Community groups should be therapeutic, inasmuch as they assist members to grow to the fullness of their life in Christ . . . People need to see a group of persons, motivated by the gospel and their love

of God, who live in such a way that loneliness and alienation are dispelled".[5]

J. Jeffrey Means notes that "the church [should] be a place that offers care and support to those who have been hurt by violence or abuse . . . . And the church [should] offer an environment of healing for those elements within people that set them up to interact with others in hurtful ways".[6]

Levels of healing will occur as the saints experience the eating and drinking of Christ together. But specific matters are often best handled in ongoing body life in appropriate ways. I'm not talking about "fixing" people and their problems, but coming along side as an encouragement to others, and letting the Lord bring about His purposes.

Henri Nouwen points out that we all have the privilege of being part of the healing process:

"We are all healers who can reach out to offer health, and we are all patients in constant need of help . . . . Healing means, first of all, the creation of an empty but friendly space where those who suffer can tell their story to someone who can listen with real attention . . . . We can do much more for each other than we often are aware of . . . . A general atmosphere of careful attention by all the members of the Christian community can sometimes heal wounds before special care is demanded".[7]

Sensitivity to One Another
We all know that Christmas trees and Easter eggs have split churches. In Romans 14 and 15 Paul points Jewish and Gentile believers to Jesus Christ as the One who accepts us, and therefore we are to accept one another. The kingdom of God is not about eating and drinking, but about living in the Spirit.

The ever-present problem is that people make something huge out of nothing. In Paul's day this happened with circumcision. He said, coming out of a Jewish background, that in Christ "circumcision was nothing." But false teachers wanted to make it a big issue. Here's the important question. Why did Paul allow Timothy to be circumcised, but not Titus? One was a case of serving others, the other was a case of legalism. Because of his partial Gentile background, Timothy was circumcised in order to reach out with the Gospel to Jews. When false teachers were insisting on the need for circumcision, then Paul said a resolute "No!" to Titus's potential circumcision. Vital point: with matters that are "nothing," you can go either way with them, depending on discernment in the specific circumstances.

Another area of vast confusion is what the New Testament means by the word "offended." The Pharisees were "offended" when Jesus violated their rules and traditions, but He did not apologize to them for His actions. Paul means something very different and very specific when he speaks of "offending" another believer. He has in view "weaker" persons who cannot do certain things in faith.

For example, Paul says that there is nothing inherently wrong with the meat offered to idols in the marketplace, but some believers did not have that knowledge and thus could not eat such fare without violating their conscience. So, Paul says that if you put such meat in front of the weaker person, you "offend" them and sin against Christ. If it cannot be eaten in faith by them, they sin by partaking of it.

Conscience

It is our responsibility to be sensitive to believers around us. If we know that certain folks came out of religious groups which taught that coffee, tea, alcoholic drinks, etc., were taboo, then we need to be careful that we do not draw them into partaking of things which violate their conscience. If we do so, then we are causing an "offense."

We must understand that the conscience operates on information received, whether correct or misinformed. If a person has been taught from diapers up that it is a sin not to meet with others on the Sabbath (Saturday), you can understand why they would balk at you inviting them to gather with your friends on another day. As such people learn of Christ and the New Covenant, then hopefully they will see that Jesus is our Sabbath, and that all foods/drinks are fine. This does not mean that they have to drink coffee or necessarily change their diet, but it does mean they will see that there is nothing wrong with others eating/drinking the way they do.

This is why we must be very sensitive to the consciences of others, and why we must seek to have our consciences informed by Christ, not by false information.

This is a crucial point: Christ does not ask us to knuckle under to the whims of religious Pharisees, but we are to go out of our way not to put stumbling blocks in the way of weaker brothers and sisters.

Looking at Ourselves in the Mirror

In light of what I have shared in this article, would it not be healthy for a group to come into the presence of Jesus and one another and candidly respond to such questions as these?

- Do we have an open, welcoming atmosphere in which all feel safe in sharing their portion of Christ?

- Have there been occasions when some contributions have been silenced by being put down or intimidated? As Frank Viola pointed out, when we gaze into the eyes of another believer, we are looking at Christ. Remember, then, if we demean or are rude to a brother or sister, we are speaking/acting directly to our Lord.

- Do all feel that their voices have been encouraged, solicited, listened to, considered and incorporated in the decision-making process?

- Does the group feel like they are moving together, not acting on anything until His peace descends on all of them with one-mindedness, or is there a sense that at times things are pressured and rushed through?

• Is care taken to make sure that communication of body issues has reached everyone, and that time has been given for questions, exploration and clarification to take place?

• Do the brothers and sisters feel that Christ's leadership is being expressed freely through everyone, or is it defaulting over time to some in the body?

• Does each believer display through Christ in them that they are eager to hear and respond to the concerns, the perspectives, the voice and the heart of every brother and sister?

• How can we expect to discover the Lord's mind in our midst if we do not honor, defer to, and submit to our Christ in each other?

• When the sun goes down, if all voices are not solicited, heard and duly considered, the will of Christ will remain unknown to that group. Anything that hinders the free expression of all voices must be challenged. When a group is told, "If you disagree and most everyone else agrees, keep silent! In time the Lord will change your mind to how the group at large feels. Your hesitation only stops the flow of what the Lord is doing," the Spirit of God is grieved. The history of church and society show that the minority are often right. Further, we listen to those we love, so no one should be told to keep silent—every voice is vital, and could be the voice of Christ to the body.[8]

Bulls-Eye Summary by T. Austin Sparks

The following remarks by T. Austin Sparks crisply capture the burdens that have been expressed in my article. Please take them to our Father and see what He would say to you.

Christ in you, the hope of glory. (Colossians 1:27)

What does this mean? Not that I come before God saying, "I have had pure motives; I have been very honest, earnest and conscientious, and my intentions have all been of the best." Let us stop talking nonsense. It is utter folly to talk like that. We do not know ourselves. Only God knows the truth about us, and none of that finds a place with Him or counts with Him for a moment. The point is, have I recognized that the Cross of the Lord Jesus was the smashing and ending of me, good and bad, so that I am not holding up before the Lord anything? I am as capable of the worst as any being in God's creation is. For anybody to take the attitude that they are not capable of the worst is an attitude of the deepest deception. We do not know the power in our beings until we are put to it. If we have never committed the worst, it is because we have never been put to it in the mercy of God, but it is all there. The Lord puts His finger upon it in principle when He says, "He that hates his brother is a murderer." It is the same spirit. You have only to extend that, provoke that anger enough, put that nature into certain circumstances, and you will discover that you are capable of things of which you would have stood in utmost horror at one time.

You and I have got to come down before God and admit that we are capable of the worst, not standing on the ground of our right. The only right one is Christ from God's standpoint. The only safe one is Christ, and therefore the only one who stands in God's eyes is Christ, and it is as you and I, in all the brokenness, frailty, conscious weakness and humility of our own beings, by faith cling to Christ that we shall find the way out, the deliverance, the salvation. We must look behind God's words to see bigger things than words on the surface indicate. "To this person will I look, even to him that is poor and of a contrite spirit, and that trembles at My word." That statement embodies all that we are saying. To what one will He look? To the one who never says, "I am right!" but to the one who says, "I may be as wrong as ever a man or woman was wrong, there is nothing of which I am not capable; my

only ground is Christ; so help me God, Christ is my ground!"
To stand on Christ is to stand always in the consciousness
and recognition that this other ground, ourselves at any point,
is dangerous ground. He is so Other, and there is the great
divide, there is no overlapping. Between Christ and us there is
a gaping chasm. God never sees that bridged, but thank God
He will put Christ into us by the Holy Spirit, and while the
two will ever remain apart, the old creation will go one day
and that which is of Christ, as wrought into us, will abide.[9] ■

1. Frank Viola, *From Eternity to Here*, David C. Cook, 2009, excerpts from pages 233-305

2. Conversation from Facebook, July 2014

3. Nathan Lee, "Bring Down the Fire," Risk Everything

4. Larry Crabb, *Encouragement: The Key to Caring*, Zondervan, 1984, pages 84, 91

5. Hammett & Sofield, *Searching Together, 24:3*, 1996, pages 2-4

6. J. Jeffrey Means, *Trauma & Evil: Healing the Wounded Soul*, Fortress Press, 2000

7. Henri Nouwen, *Reaching Out*, Doubleday, 1975

8. Expanded thoughts from the "Consensus" Break-Out at Interconnect, July, 2013, Nashville that appeared in Jon Zens' blog, December, 2014, www.searchingtogether. org/blog

9. T. Austin-Sparks, *The Church of the Firstborn*, Chapter 1

Books for further reading

• Emil Brunner, *The Misunderstanding of the Church*, 1952

• Vernard Eller, *The Outward Bound: Caravaning as the Style of the Church*, Eerdmans, 1980

• S.D. Gaede, *Belonging: Our Need for Community in Church & Family*, Zondervan, 1985

• Milt Rodriguez, *The Community Life of God*

• Frank Viola, *The Re-Thinking Series*, http://frankviola.org/rethinkingseries/

• Jon Zens, *58 to 0—How Christ Leads Through the One Anothers*

• Jon Zens, *A Church Building Every ½ Mile: What Makes American Christianity Tick?*

• Jon Zens, *The Pastor Has No Clothes: Moving from Clergy-Centered Church to Christ-Centered Ekklesia*

THE MISTAKEN IDENTITY OF GOD'S WORD WRITTEN

DENNIS J. MULKEY

Best-selling Christian author and New Testament scholar-theologian, N.T. Wright, has insightfully noted that:

> As the church, within its own life and proclamation, uses *a scriptural word or concept* but denotes by that word or concept something more than, or even different from, what is meant by the word or concept *in its scriptural origin,* three effects are almost inevitable. First, it will then *misread Scripture at that point,* imagining that when the Bible uses that word it is talking about the thing which the church normally talks about when it uses that word....Second, such a reading will *miss completely the thing that Scripture was talking about at that point....*Third, *it will imagine itself to have biblical warrant for its own ideas,* when all it actually has are 'biblical echoes' of its own voice [emphasis mine].[1]

This I take to be a wise warning about attaching the wrong *meaning* to "a scriptural word or concept" because of three serious consequences that will likely follow. I'm convinced that what N.T. Wright warns us about has actually occurred with regard to the meaning of the terms "Word of God," "Word of the Lord" and "the Word" throughout the New Testament (NT). Whenever any of these three terms "in its scriptural origin" is believed to denote *the Bible,* a serious *misreading* of its *true* meaning has occurred; further (a la Wright), the Spirit-intended *meaning* of that biblical passage will have been *missed* altogether, and (finally) each time any of these three phrases is read or heard, the *mistaken* meaning instantly associated with them—namely, that each refers to "the Bible"—will be simply presumed and thereby reinforced in our minds even more so.

Examine the following three NT passages from the NASB, paying close attention to the *italicized* phrases:

> And when they had prayed, the place where they had gathered together was shaken, and they were all filled with the Holy Spirit and began to speak *the Word of God* with boldness.[2]

> So when they had solemnly testified and spoken *the Word of the Lord,* they started back to Jerusalem, and were preaching the gospel to many villages of the Samaritans.[3]

> But we will devote ourselves to prayer and to the ministry of *the Word.*[4]

In each of three NT passages cited above, the term "Word" appearing in *"the Word of God," "the Word of the Lord,"* and *"the Word"* refers specifically and exclusively to the Gospel Message of Jesus Christ and not at all to the Bible! A thorough investigation using an exhaustive Bible concordance will also reveal that never once does the NT link the term "Word" *(logos)* synonymously with the term "Scripture" (in either its singular or plural form) whenever the latter term appears in the New Testament over 50 times.

Use of the same concordance will reveal that the term "Word" (when referring to the divine *message* for the NT era) denotes only the Gospel of Christ in its propositional form.[5] This one and only *apostolic meaning* of the verbalized Word of God has been subtly and subversively compromised within biblical Christianity. How so? By identifying the 66 books of "all Scripture" as the very Word of God *alongside* the Gospel of Christ. Instead of one God-given identity for his everlasting Word—that of the Gospel of Christ—a second one has been posited and introduced—that of the canon of the biblical Scriptures. The outcome is that of the "double exposure effect" evident in the creation of blended images: two or more separate and distinct photos/images are blended synthetically together to create an image that is in fact *only* the outcome of human ingenuity and technology.[6] It is not the authentic representation (or real reflection) of a bit of reality outside the human mind captured in a photo at a particular moment and place.

By whose authority and in whose name dare Bible-believing Christians tamper with and taint the clear NT revelation that the Gospel of Christ *alone* is the one and only, divinely-intended meaning of God's Word in our NT era? How is it now that to be considered truly "orthodox" within evangelical Christianity one *must* believe and confess that the Word of God in its verbal (propositional) form is to be understood as referring to "the 66 Books of the Bible" when it *never* did so originally in the NT text?

How is it that a distinctly different identity for the Word of God, namely that of the Bible (or "all Scripture"), might subtly arise in biblical Christianity? Primarily it seems to have come from a bit of simple logic and human reasoning, permitted to override and contradict explicit New Testament revelation. It seems so naturally logical and reasonable to identify "all Scripture" as the very "Word of God" when it is affirmed (rightly, I believe!) that the former has been wholly "inspired by God" (as per 2 Tim. 3:16). There appears to have been an unchecked logical leap that took (and continues to take) some form like this: "Since 'all Scripture' *is* 'God-breathed' then it *must be* the very Word of God!" The problem though is that this new, post-apostolic identity for the Word conflicts clearly with that revealed in the "God-breathed" NT writings themselves; as I have noted, they clearly identify the Word of God for our present (NT) era as that *alone* of the totality of the Gospel propositions *connected* to the living Lord Jesus Christ.[7]

Truth is that *both* "the Bible" and "the Gospel" *cannot* be the true identity of the one and only Word of God. They are simply *not* synonyms for each other. All the doctrines of the Gospel are found in the Bible but not all the doctrines of the Bible are found in the Gospel. The biblical Scriptures of the Old and New Testaments contain doctrines and duties *other than* those alone comprising the Gospel of our Lord Jesus. They include onetime "truths" that were intended only for Israel, pertaining to the Law of Moses and prior to the arrival of the Messiah Jesus, as instanced throughout the book of Hebrews. And they include various *applications* of the Word of the Gospel that were clearly intended for a bygone era and culture, as instanced in 1 Corinthians 11:2-16.

By mistakenly identifying the Bible as *God's Word Written,* Christians can easily conclude that any specific Scripture counsel must be taken as the "Word of God" for them, when in fact this may not be so in our present NT era. We can be easily seduced into preoccupation with obeying principles and imitating practices and pursuing patterns present in the Bible that do not belong at all to the living Christ revealed in the Gospel. The Word of God in its verbalized, written form is to be confined exclusively to *only those truths* comprising the unsearchable riches of Jesus Christ. Where are we to find these truths? Only in the divine revelation infallibly *recorded* in the 66 Books of the Bible! The canon of "All Scripture" alone is to be regarded as the finally authoritative *source-book* for any and all truth about our Lord Jesus Christ. Every truth of the Word of the Gospel (Acts 15:7) must be derived from and grounded in the unfolding biblical revelation that culminated in the apostolic writings of the New Testament.[8]

According to the climactic revelation of the New Testament, we Christians should be pursuing continual fellowship with the Person of Jesus Christ who is the Lord of all and our Eternal Life, who by his very own Spirit really indwells us. Truth is that as often as we *come to* and *commune with* the living Christ of the biblical Gospel, he *communicates* his victorious life to and through us. We need not be distracted by the lie that preoccupation with the Christ of the Scripture rather than the Scripture of Christ is dangerous, perhaps even deadly to and for us! What is especially dangerous and deadly for us is being under the spell of a non-biblical, false identity for God's Word, one that subtly and continually lures us away from an all-consuming love affair with the all-sufficient Christ!

A dual identity for the Word of God as that of both the biblical Canon and the biblical Christ tends to diminish Christian preoccupation with Jesus Christ *alone* as our wholly sufficient Savior and life. The Canon of Scripture and the Christ of Scripture are not synonyms! Christian author James Fowler captures the quintessence of authentic biblical Christianity in the following statements:

> When Jesus thus dwells and reigns spiritually in those who receive Him by faith, the kingdom that Jesus so often referred to becomes operative. The resurrection-life of Jesus becomes the spiritual empowering of the Christian's life and participation in the ecclesia of the Church. Such a spiritual, gospel reality of "Christianity" can only be defined as the dynamic life and activity of the living Lord Jesus Christ. Christianity is Christ!....Indeed, the intrinsic unity of the physically incarnated Jesus and the resurrected, ascended Jesus poured out in the form of the Spirit of Christ on Pentecost, continuing to function in every age and unto eternity in the expression of His own Being, must be maintained unequivocally as the essence of Christianity.[9]

Yes, authentic Christianity—biblically grounded and revealed Christianity—is that alone of the *living* Lord Jesus Christ living out his very own life in, as and through those who love him sincerely. Leonard Sweet and Frank Viola contend ever so rightly (in my view) in one of their recent co-authored books, *Jesus Manifesto,* that

> ...the major disease of today's church is JDD: Jesus Deficit Disorder....When we dethrone Jesus Christ from his rightful place, we tarnish the face of Christianity and redefine it out

of existence. Can our problems really be caused by something so basic and simple as losing sight of Christ? We believe the answer is a resounding *Yes* [italics theirs].[10]

My response to these words is an unhesitating, "Yea and Amen!"[11]

Once again, I pose the question, how is it that a distinctly *different* identity for the "Word of God" (namely, that of *the Bible*) might arise in addition to the *only* one which the New Testament presumes and presents repeatedly (namely, that of *the Gospel of Christ*)? One likely reason I noted earlier was that of unwittingly allowing human logic and reasoning to subtly prevail over clear NT revelation. I believe there is yet another subversive intervening reason, one that lies behind the misuse of human reason and that needs the full spotlight. Might there not have been a secret, subtle and sustained satanic *prompting* to fall prey to such human logic, akin to what happened in the Primordial Garden with our First Parents? This seems especially likely in light of the deeply ironic "anti-Christ" consequences stemming from the intrusion of a competing *biblical* identity for the Word of God.

Focusing more upon the Bible than upon the Christ of the Bible would effectively mean failure to give Jesus Christ "first place in everything" (Col. 1:18) that he so rightly deserves. It tends to mask the truth that our Lord and Life is to be our all and all (Col. 3:11), since "in Him the fullness of Deity dwells in bodily form" (Col. 2:9) and in Him *only* are we "made complete" (Col. 2:10). Who might obviously be most interested in dishonoring Christ and diluting our devotion to him? None other than the very "father of lies" (John 8:44) whom Jesus utterly defeated once and for all at Calvary! It is so like the Devil to masquerade as an angel of light (2 Cor. 11:3, 14), using something perfectly good ("All Scripture") to subtly subvert the *Gospel-only* contents of the matured Word of God, thereby luring sincere Christians away from an otherwise full devotion to their Savior and Lord! DeVern

Fromke, in his *No Other Foundation,* illumines clearly this dark reality in these comments:

> When Satan slipped into the garden to turn Adam and Eve aside, he could not accomplish his design without the help of something that was seemingly very good, necessary and important. We know that God wanted Adam to live from the *tree of life,* a tree which actually represented God Himself, as all that was necessary for accomplishing life's true goal and purpose. But Satan was there enticing man to accept knowledge, not as God would impart it from Himself, but as it could be received through this "other tree" – the tree of knowledge.
>
> Let me emphasize just how good and how deceptive this offer still is today. We might paraphrase it in this word picture: In my mind's eye I can almost see Satan holding out the Bible and saying, "Here, let me show you the underlying principles of life; in this Book you will uncover the hidden patterns for successful living; let me help you search out the deep purposes and meaning of life."
>
> How strange this sounds to us! We can hardly imagine that Satan would suggest a substitute way – that of *using the Bible differently than God intended.* Yet he is actually holding out the Bible as the "tree of knowledge" for fallen man to use in running his own life and realizing his own pursuits. We must hasten to say, just here, that *God has never intended for His children to use the Bible thus;* rather He has purposed that [through it]…He might reveal Himself in Jesus Christ.[12]

It seems clear to me that a *presumed* identity for "the Word of God" as that of "the Bible" is rooted in a satanic scheme of "using the Bible differently than God intended" it to be. Though it is possible to rigorously and faithfully pursue "Christ-only-ness" while believing that *both* the Bible *and* the Gospel of Jesus Christ are the Word of God, there is an overwhelming gravitational pull away from focusing always upon Christ alone as our Life; instead we tend to focus upon biblical principles, practices and patterns *unconnected* to the living Christ. Why? Because we have mistakenly perceived them to be part of the revealed Word of God *alongside of and in addition to* the Gospel of Christ!

The Bible preserves all essential and infallible truths of the Gospel; the contents of its 66 books include a fully trustworthy account of the Gospel's historically unfolding revelation, and its last 27 books (i.e., the NT portion) authoritatively and clearly pinpoints the Gospel of Christ *alone* as the one and only divinely-intended identity of the Word of God. The renowned 20th Century New Testament Scholar, F. F. Bruce spotlighted this truth of the Gospel of Christ as the final and full Message God intends for us all in the following words:

> All the successive acts and varying modes of revelation in the ages before Christ came did not add up to the fullness of what God had to say. His was not completely uttered until Christ came; but when Christ came, the word spoken in Him was indeed God's final word. In Him all the promises of God meet with the answering, "Yes!" which seals their fulfillment to His people and evokes from them an answering "Amen!" The story of divine revelation is a story of progression up to Christ, but there is no progression beyond Him...God's previous spokesmen were His servants, but for the proclamation of His last word to man He has chosen His Son...He [Christ, the Son] is the Prophet through whom God has spoken His final word to men; He is the Priest who has accomplished a perfect work of cleansing for His people's sins; He is the King who sits enthroned in the place of chief honor alongside the Majesty on high...The authority of the gospel...was the authority of Jesus, the Son of God, supremely exalted by His Father. As God had no greater messenger than His Son, He had no further message beyond the gospel.[13]

The only way forward is for biblical Christianity to realign with the apostolic revelation of the New Testament. We must perceive and preserve the distinctly different divine purposes for the Bible *and* for the Word of God identified. The Bible is to be identified as the divinely-inspired, fully authoritative written Record of the

Word of God. It includes the historical progression of this Word of God that culminated in the revelation of its one and only identity as that of the Gospel of Christ.

The *Living* Word of God is the Lord Jesus Christ and the *Written* Word of God is divinely *delimited* to the summation of every verbalized truth about our Lord, each of which *must be* shown to have been derived from the Bible in order for it to be rightly included as part of the authentic and eternal Word of God (Rev. 14:6; 1 Pet. 1:23, 25). The divinely-intended relationship between the Scripture *and* the Word of God is succinctly pinpointed in Acts 8.35: "Philip opened his mouth and beginning from this Scripture he preached Jesus to him." ∎

---

1. N.T. Wright, *Justification: God's Plan and Paul's Vision* (Downers Grove: InterVarsity Press, 2009), 81.

2. Acts 4:31, italics and capitalized "W" in "Word" is for emphasis; see also: Acts 6:7; 8:14; 11:1; 13:5, 46; 2 Cor. 4:2; Phil. 1:14; Col. 1:25; 1 Thess. 2:13; 2 Tim. 2:8-9; 1 Pet. 1:23.

3. Acts 8:25, italics and capitalized "W" in "Word" is for emphasis; see also: Acts 12:24; 13:44, 48-49; 16:32; 19:10; 1 Thess. 1:8; 2 Thess. 3:1; 1 Pet. 1:25.

4. Acts 6:4, italics and capitalized "W" in "Word" is for emphasis; see also: Acts 10:36; 11:19; 16:6; 17:11; 18:5; 1 Cor. 15:2; 1 Thess. 1:6; 1 Pet. 1:25.

5. Several examples of the clear New Testament intent to use the terms "word" *(logos)* and "gospel" synonymously are the following: Acts 20:24, 32; 1 Thess. 1:5-6; 2:9, 13; Phil. 1:12-14; 2 Tim. 2:8-9 and 1 Pet 1:23, 25.

6. "Double Exposure Photography: 50+ Examples and Tutorials" at: http://www.hongkiat.com/blog/double-multiple-exposure-photography-tutorials/ (accessed 6/15/15).

7. See Part I of my book, *Treason Against Christ: A Summons to Reclaim the Authentic Identity of the Word of God,* for a detailed presentation and discussion of this topic.

8. See the final chapter of Part I—"The Monarch Butterfly, the Old Testament Era and the Word of God"—in my book, *Treason Against Christ,* in which I propose that the developmental stage-forms of the butterfly seem to aptly illustrate the unfolding, progressively maturing stage-forms of the Word of God culminating in the Gospel of Christ.

9. James Fowler, "Christianity is Christ," http://christinyou.net/pages/sntyisxst.html (accessed 2/8/15).

10. Leonard Sweet and Frank Viola, *Jesus Manifesto: Restoring the Supremacy and Sovereignty of Jesus Christ* (Nashville: Thomas Nelson, 2010), xviii-xix.

11. The allegation of "Jesus Deficit Disorder" (JDD) as the disease which hallmarks today's Evangelical Church seems undeniably insightful and accurate to me. It is precisely what I am attempting to pinpoint and spotlight through the present title of my own book— *Treason Against Christ: A Summons to Reclaim the Authentic Identity of the Word of God.* My intent was to allure (attract) interest in its message, never to wag a condemning finger at my fellow brothers and sisters in Christ! I do intend (if our Lord permits) to publish a Second Edition that will include a rearrangement of some chapter contents and their sequential ordering, etc., as well as a new title such as: *Living by the Living Christ: Moving from Chrysalis to Butterfly,* first suggested by my darling daughter, Anna Deborah Giocondo, M.D.

12. DeVern Fromke, *No Other Foundation* (Elkhart, IN: Strategic Press, N.D.), 168. Italics in this citation are mine, for emphasis only. Apparently the book was originally published in 1965, then re-published at a later unrevealed date "with the author's permission" by Strategic Press, with this note: "We have edited and abridged it slightly." For more, see www.LivingFaithBooks.com.

13. F. F. Bruce, *The Epistle to the Hebrews: The English Text with Introduction, Exposition and Notes* (Grand Rapids: Eerdmans, 1970), 3, 8, 26.

ALL THINGS IN CHRIST

T. AUSTIN-SPARKS

We take the Epistles and we think of them as having to do within the building of the Church and the churches, the superstructure of Christianity, and so we take the technique of the Acts and the Epistles as a technique, as a system of doctrine and a system of practice, a system of Christian order, and the Epistles become—and have become for so many and for Christianity in general— a crystallized system of practice, order, form, teaching; and the weakness in the whole position is just this, that that is something as in itself and the Lord Jesus has just been missed and lost.

I wonder if you detect what I mean by that? You see, the Holy Spirit' S way is to take Christ and open up Christ, to the heart, and show that Christ is a heavenly order; not that the Epistles set forth as a manual a heavenly order, but that Christ is that order, and everything in the matter of order has to be kept immediately in relation to the living Person. If it becomes some thing, then it becomes an earthly system; and you can make out of the Epistles a hundred different earthly systems all built upon the Epistles. They will support any number of different systems, different interpretations, represented by Christian orders here, and the reason is that they have been divorced from the Person.

You see, beloved, there are numerous things, numerous subjects, themes, teachings. There is "the kingdom of God", there is "sanctification", there is "eternal life", there is "the victorious life", "the overcomer" or "the overcoming life", there is "the second coming of Christ". These are but a few subjects, themes, truths, as they are called, which have been taken up and developed out of the Scriptures and become things with which people have become very much occupied, and in which they are very interested as things. So certain people hive off around a sanctification teaching, and they are the sanctificationists, and it becomes an "ism". Others hive off; and they are bounded by the hedge of Second Adventism, the Lord's coming, prophecy, and all that. So you get groups like that. I want to say that would be utterly impossible if the Person of the Lord Jesus was dominant.

What is the kingdom of God? It is Christ. If you get right inside of the Gospels, you will find that the kingdom of God is Jesus Christ. If you are living in Christ, you are in the kingdom, and you know, as the Holy Spirit teaches you Christ, what the kingdom is in every detail. The kingdom is not some thing, in the first place. The kingdom, when it becomes something universal, will simply be the expression and manifestation of Christ. That is all. You come to the kingdom in and through Christ; and the same is true of everything else.

What is sanctification? It is not a doctrine. It is not an 'it' at all. It is Christ. He is made unto us sanctification (1 Cor. 1:30). If you are in Christ and if the Holy Spirit is teaching you Christ, then you are knowing all about sanctification; and if He is not, you may have a theory and doctrine of sanctification but it will separate you from other Christians, and will be bringing any number of Christians into difficulties. Probably the teaching of sanctification as a thing has brought more Christians into difficulty than any other particular doctrine, through making it a thing, instead of keeping Christ as our sanctification.

I am only saying this to try to explain...That it is in the School of Christ that we are to be found, where the Holy Spirit is not teaching us things; not Church doctrine, not sanctification, not Adventism, not any thing or any number of things, but teaching us Christ. What is Adventism? What is the coming of the Lord? Well, it is the coming of the Lord. And what is the coming of the Lord? Well, such a word as this will give us the key: He shall come to be glorified in His saints, and to be marveled at in all them that believed (2 Thess. 1:10). You see, it is the consummation of something that has been going on in an inward way. How then do I best know that the coming of the Lord draws nigh? Not best of all by prophetical signs, but by what is going on within the hearts of the Lord's people. That is the best sign of the times, namely, what the Spirit of God is doing in the people of God. But you are not interested in that. You would far sooner know what is going to happen between Germany and Russia, whether these two, after all, are going to make it up and become a great confederacy! How far does it get us? Where has all the talking about the revived Roman Empire got us? That is Adventism as a thing. If only we keep close to Him Who is the sum of all truth, and move with Him and learn Him, we shall know the course of things. We shall know what is imminent. We shall have in our heart whisperings of preparation.

The best Advent preparation is to know the Lord. I am not saying that there is nothing in prophecy; don't misunderstand me. But I do know that there are multitudes of people who are simply engrossed in prophecy as a thing whose spiritual life counts for nothing, who really have no deep inward walk with the Lord. We have seen it so often.

I shall never forget, on a visit to the United States, going into one of the big cities where I was to speak for a week. Everything was so arranged that my first message was timed to follow the last message of a man who had had a week before me, and he had been on prophecy for the whole week. I went into the last meeting where he gave his final message on the signs of the time. Notebooks were out, and they were taking it all down, fascinated. It was all external, all objective; such things as the Roman Empire revived and Palestine recovered. You know the sort of thing. Then he finished and they were waiting for some more, and the notebooks were ready. The Lord put it right into my heart that the first word was to be, "And every one that hath this hope set on Him purifieth himself, even as He is pure" (1 John 3:3); to speak on the spiritual effect of that spiritual hope. They were not interested in that. The notebooks were closed, pencils put away; there was no interest as I sought in the Lord to be very faithful as to what all this should mean in an inward way, in adjustment to the Lord, and so on. They were only longing for the meeting to close. When I finished—they hardly waited for me to finish—they were up and out. ∎

Excerpt from *The School of Christ,* Chapter 6, "An Open Heaven." First published in *A Witness and A Testimony* magazine, Mar-Apr 1943, Vol 21-2.

LOOKING FOR PAST ISSUES OF SEARCHING TOGETHER?

A full set of back issues of *Searching Together* is available for $70 postpaid.

This set consists of around 85 published issues of our quarterly Journal from 1978 to 2015, many of which consist of multiple quarters.

These Journals contain many articles opening up aspects of our life in Christ, our life together in His body, and extending grace and forgiveness to one another.

You can order this set by either:

1. Sending a check for $70 to Searching Together, PO Box 548, St Croix Falls WI 54024

2. Visiting www.searchingtogether.org and donating $70 via PayPal by clicking on the "Donate" button.

You will be built up and challenged by reading these back issues spanning our 40 year history!